Step By Step Guide on Successful Snail Farming

Step By Step Guide on Successful Snail Farming

Anthony Adefarakan

AQUATON KONSULTS

CONTENTS

INTRODUCTION

PROCUREMENT OF FOUNDATION STOCK

HOUSING OF THE SNAILS

FEEDING OF THE SNAILS

GROWTH AND REPRODUCTION IN SNAILS

MANAGEMENT PRACTICES IN SNAIL FARMING

MAKING MONEY IN SNAIL FARMING

ABOUT THE AUTHOR

INTRODUCTION

The process of farming or raising snails is scientifically referred to as Heliciculture. Snails are small soft animals, usually with a hard round shell on their back which move very slowly. They are of different types and origins. For instance, there are some which are of African origin. They include *Archachatina marginata, Achatina achatina, Achatina fulica, Limicolaria spp, Limicolaria martensis etc.* While some like *Helix aspersa, Helix aperta, Helix lucorum, Helix pomatia, Helix hortensis* etc. are European breeds.

Snails generally consist of three main parts; they are:

i. **The shell** - which constitutes 30 - 40% of the whole body. It varies in colour from one species to another and the thickness depends on the age of the snail i.e. the older the snail, the thicker the shell; and it increases as the body size increases. It is also a very good source of calcium.
ii. **The Muscular foot** — this is otherwise known as the edible portion. It constitutes about 35 - 45% of the whole body and it is the organ for locomotion.
iii. **The visceral mass** -- which comprises the internal organs such as heart, kidney, loop of intestine and reproductive organ. It constitutes about 20 -25% of the whole body and it is not eaten by man.

Snail farming is considered a good venture around the world because snail is a cheap source of animal protein and the farming is also easy to set up. Other factors supporting snail farming include the following;

1. The fat content and cholesterol level is very low compared to chicken (or poultry),

2. It is a cure for anaemia because of its high iron content,

3. The meat is a delicacy,

4. The feed is readily available,

5. The management practice is simple,

6. The shell can be used ornamentally,

7. The farming does not constitute any environmental nuisance,

8. It is not capital intensive,

9. Snail is hardy and therefore not easily predisposed to disease,

10. Snail meat is tasty, juicy and tender with good flavour.

All these factors also make snail farming a good option for anyone who is interested in making cool and sweat-less money from practicing agriculture.

Although snails of different origins have been mentioned earlier on, in this handbook, one of the African giant land snails, *Archachatina marginata* will be our focus being one of the commonest. The Yoruba's call it "Igbin Apinnu"; and it has the biggest size, even as the adult weighs between 300 -700g. The fleshy part is dark brown in colour and the shell is wider at the posterior end.

PROCUREMENT OF FOUNDATION STOCK

This refers to the ways by which snails can be obtained for the commencement of the farming. Snails can be procured through different means;

1. **Picking:** snails are known for hiding under sheds, fallen leaves, rotten banana leaves, building blocks, wet cut plants etc. during the day time due to their nocturnal nature i.e. they are mostly active in the night. So one can resolve to search for the adult snails especially in order to commence the farming. The search from experience is most productive during rainy season. To have a productive search, make use of the night especially after it has just rained (with a very bright torchlight); only be careful with some other dangerous animals sharing the same habitat with the snails.
2. **Purchasing:** This is another way by which snails can be procured. You buy good breeding stock of about 300-350g weight, selecting active ones without shell damage. This is better done during the rainy season when their prices are relatively cheap. Purchased snails are to be transported in a well-ventilated condition (not in the booth of a car for instance) and it has to be early in the morning or late in the evening. They must be gently handled for effective performance.
3. **Other means**- which include being given, inherited stock etc.

But in any case, the procured snails are to be placed under close surveillance for about 2-3 days, checking and observing their behaviour. If they fare well, you can move them into their prepared pen, but if any of them is suspected to be diseased, isolate it from others so that its condition will not affect the other snails; especially if the disease is infectious. Ensure your snails are all fine before you put them together in the same pen.

HOUSING OF THE SNAILS

Snails can be raised in various forms of pens and enclosures, depending on the scale of production — whether small or large scale.

For instance, old tires, tanks and drums can be used for small scale production. Starters can begin with these, even as little or no capital is required for setting them up. Building blocks can also be arranged in a rectangular form with wire netting reinforced with mosquito net as covering. These kinds of housing will however only be able to raise small number of snails.

On the other hand, cages (metallic or wooden) and fenced pens (high or low) are good housing types for both small and large scale production. They can be made with affordable and durable materials. However, it should be ensured that the wire netting used for the pen is well reinforced with mosquito net so as to prevent baby snails from escaping and at the same time protect the snails against predators like snake, lizard, rats etc.

A recommended stocking rate for a standard pen is:
- Hatchling or Baby snail   -   40 - 50 snails/m^2
- Growers   -   35- 40 snails/m^2
- Adult or Breeding snail   -   10 – 15 snails/m^2

FEEDING OF THE SNAILS

Many people have wondered how snails feed. Well, it is one of the wonders of God. Snails eat by rasping the feed with their radula. The radula is a delicate tooth-like projection, having the likeness of homodont dentition and it can only be seen when the snail is feeding, most especially in the night or when it rains. They prefer succulent feed due to the nature of their radula.

Snails feed on varieties of feeds; these include:

1. Fruits of mango, banana, plantain, orange, bread fruit, carrot, cucumber, ripe pears, tomatoes, pumpkins etc.
2. Leaves of cocoyam, banana, cassava, guava, sweet potato, pawpaw, onion greens, hibiscus, lettuce, spinach etc. They prefer juicy leaves to dry ones.
3. Sweet potato and yam (cooked or raw), beans, corn (cooked or raw) etc.
4. Agricultural by-products — rice bran, wheat offal, palm kernel cake, soya beans residue, peels of plantain, banana, pawpaw, cocoyam etc.
5. Dry ground cereals -maize, groundnut cake, soya bean, wheat and sorghum.
6. Mineral supplements -ground oyster shell, bone meal, limestone, ground snail shell etc.
7. Compounded ration — well ground broiler starter mash, layer mash and grower mash provided as supplement diet. As a matter of fact, two types of feed that snails like and also promote good growth are (a) broiler finisher mash consisting of 7%

broiler concentrate, 58% corn, 16% soya, 18% sorghum, 7% limestone, flour (40% Ca), and (b) chicken feed (pellets) for layers consisting of 5% layer concentrate, 50% corn, 15%soya, 20% sorghum, 44% barley, 6%limestone flour (40% Ca). Fish meal and blood meal are also good protein supplements in feeding the snails.

8. Water – this should be provided in a shallow container to reduce the risk of the snail drowning. Chlorinated or dirty water should be avoided. Rain, borehole or well water is preferable. It must also be ensured that the snails have easy access to enough water especially when fed with dry mash.

Factors Affecting Feeding In Snails

Feeding activity in snails can be enhanced by some factors, these include:

1. Freshness of the feed

2. Feed with low fiber content

3. Succulence and fineness of the feed

4. Availability and easy access to drinking water especially when fed with dry mash.

5. Considerably high relative humidity, moderate temperature, fairly dark condition of the pen, food   preference versus food supplied etc.

6. Snails also feed well when the feed is moist.

It is however worthy of note that since the feeding activity to a considerably large
extent depends on the weather, snails may not necessarily feed every day. This should not raise too much an alarm. Just ensure that you simulate the conditions obtainable in the

wild right in the pen so that their habitat requirements (especially for feeding) will not be totally altered. Let the snails feel as if they are still in their natural states in the forest.

Take note of these facts when feeding the snails;

1. Weight gain is directly proportional to the level of feed intake,
2. Shell growth is directly proportional to the feed intake, and
3. The size of the snail is directly proportional to the digestibility of the feed served.
   Thus, for good and favourable performance of your snails, give quality attention to feeding them well.

GROWTH AND REPRODUCTION IN SNAILS

Growth is one of the characteristics of living things, and because snails are living things, they exhibit growth.

Under proper and ideal management, snails grow in this order:

Hatchlings   --------------   Growers   -------------   Adults

In hatchings, the shell size depends on the egg size since the shell develops from the egg's surface membrane. As the snail grows, the shell is added onto in increments. Eventually, the shell will develop a flare or reinforcing lip at its opening. This shows that the snail is now mature; there will be no further shell growth.

Growth is measured by shell size, since a snail's body weight varies and fluctuates even in 100% humidity. The growth rate varies considerably between individuals in each population group. Adult size which is related to the growth rate also varies, thus the fastest growers are usually the largest snails. Eggs grow larger, healthier snails also tend to grow faster and thus larger.

Factors Influencing Growth in Snails

Several factors can greatly influence the growth of snails. These include:

- **Population Density** – when snails are over stocked or over populated, growth is inhibited. It will result in competition which in turn will negatively affect the snails' growth.

- **Stress** – snails are sensitive to light, noise, vibration, unsanitary conditions, irregular feeding, being touched etc. All these constitute stress to the snails and they have adverse effects on their growth.

- **Feed** – conventional snail feeds like pawpaw, cocoyam and other waste products should be supplemented with compounded ration with high levels of protein and calcium to improve growth.

- **Temperature and Moisture**- when the temperature is too high, growth is adversely affected, while it is favourably enhanced when moisture or humidity is high (although not too high). High temperature with low humidity will cause delay in snail growth as dryness inhibits growth and even stops activity. When it becomes too hot or dry, the snail becomes inactive, seals its shell and aestivates i.e. becomes dormant until cooler, moister weather condition returns.

- **The breeding technology used**- Reproduction on the other hand occurs in snails on attainment of sexual maturity. The maturity age is between 8 – 12 months and it depends on the management. It is however noteworthy that snails are hermaphrodites i.e. they possess both male and female reproductive organs although they must mate with another snail of the same species (after courtship) before they lay eggs. Mating occurs both in dry and rainy seasons under proper management. Some snails may act as males one season and as females the next while others play both roles at once and fertilize each other simultaneously. After mating, the snail can store sperm received up to a year, but it usually lays eggs within a few weeks. It has been observed that snails are sometimes uninterested in mating with another snail of the same species that originated from a considerable distance way. They need sandy loam soil for laying as dry soil or too heavy soil is not suitable for the laying. If the soil is too hard the snails will be unable to bury their eggs, and as a result the eggs will be laid on the surface of the soil. Alter laying, the snail covers the hole with a moisture of the slime it secretes and dirt. This slime, which the snail secretes to help it crawl and to help preserve the moisture in its body is glycoprotein, similar to egg white.

The eggs are laid within 1-2 minutes and they are laid once. The clutch size i.e. the number of eggs laid at once ranges between 4 – 18eggs and the incubation period i.e. the time it takes for the eggs to hatch from the time of laying is between 25 – 32 days.

After laying, snails lose substantial weight, like 5-8% of the total body weight and as a result more nutritious and balanced feed should be given to the snails during this stage so as not to lose them.

The hatchability of the eggs however depends on soil temperature, soil humidity, soil composition etc. The recommended and advisable temperature and soil moisture content suitable for hatchability are 25 - 28°C and about 75% respectively. The size,
weight, shell, length, width and thickness of the hatchlings depend on the size of the "mother' i.e. the parent snail. The weight of the hatchling of *Archachatina marginata* for instance is between 2 and 7g depending on the size of the adult or "mother" snail.

The hatchlings under suitable conditions of the soil i.e. a sandy loam and well tilled soil emerge or come up 1 or 2 days after hatching. It is however noteworthy that the number of days it takes for a "baby" snail to emerge or climb to the surface of the soil after hatching depends on the hardness of the soil .If the soil is too hard i.e. not loose, the baby snail could die or take longer time to come to the surface.

Although snails could live up to 8 –9 years, after 3 years the reproductive performance in terms of egg laying, egg size and hatchling size will reduce. So there is no point keeping snails up to 9 years except for experimental purposes.

MANAGEMENT PRACTICES IN SNAIL FARMING

These refer to the various things that must be done in order to have successful snail farming. If the snails must be sustained for effective production, these practices are inevitable:

- Snails of the same breed (same species) are to be reared together.
- Adults, growers and baby snails are not to be reared together in the same pen.
- Over stocking and under stocking should be avoided.
- Adequate shade should be provided for the snailery.
- The soil if dry is to be wetted early in the morning and later in the evening.
- The snails are to be washed once in a month with clean water and not with any soap or chemical.
- Left over feeds are to be removed or packed before giving fresh ones.
- Fermented, mouldy or salty feed must be kept away from the snails.
- The soil is to be turned regularly (with care) for proper egg laying and easy emergence of baby snails from the soil.
- The conventional feeds (like leaves and fruits) should be supplemented with wet balanced diet (compounded feed with

the nutrients in adequate proportions). You can check section 4.0 for details on this.
- The snails are to be protected against solider ants' infestation.
- The rearing environment must be kept clean.
- Chemicals like insecticides must not be used in the snailery.
- It must be ensured that the housing type used is intact.
- The wire netting used for the pen should be reinforced with mosquito net in order to prevent baby snails from escaping and at the same time protect the snails against predators like snake, rats, and lizards. The nets should however be checked daily to be sure they are still intact.
- In case of any mortality, remove the dead snail(s) from the stock.
- Snails gathered from the wild to stock a snail farm may have a high mortality rate as they adjust to the new conditions. These snails may already be diseased as they may have consumed poison baits, agricultural chemicals, or poisonous plants; therefore, they should not be immediately stocked. They should be put in a separate pen and fed for at least 3 days to purge their system of any toxins and to give them chance to die if they have consumed a lethal dose. If they are still healthy after 3 – 4 days, they should be alright for stocking. Feed is to be withheld, except water for the last 1 – 2 days.
- Start snail farming with lesser number of snails i.e. practice on a small scale before embarking on a large scale production.
- Keep the entrance (door) of your snailery closed, and discourage visitors from entering the snailery.
- Keep adequate records of the snails. Carry out a daily observation and note their behaviours to feeding, drinking, to one another, to a particular feed type etc. Be very close to the snails. Create time for them.
- Cull your snails for sale during dry season or festive periods. It is wiser that way.

These should be faithfully observed for successful snail farming. There is yet another occurrence in snail farming called **Cannibalism**. It is a condition whereby snails feed on one another and it is usually caused by overstocking, poor quality or quantity of feed, and rearing of adults and hatchlings together. To prevent or correct this therefore, the factors causing it should be corrected.

MAKING MONEY IN SNAIL FARMING

If your aim or reason for engaging in snail fanning is for generating monetary benefits i.e. making money, then this section is for you.

There is no organized market for snails in this country and they are not weighed before selling. Thus, the price of snails in the market depends on the bargaining ability of the buyer, season, festivity, location and urgent need of the farmer. Due to the fact that most of the snails in the market are picked or hunted for by hunters, passers-by and hired labour in the field, the price of snails reared by farmers are always more expensive than the ones purchased from hunters or hawkers. During the rainy season, the price of snails is low because it is readily available in the bush while the price is always higher during the dry season. It is therefore advisable for farmers to sell their snails during the dry season or festive periods like Christmas, Easter, New Year, or any of the festive periods.

In selling the snails, it is better to avoid middlemen and sell directly to individuals, restaurants, hotels among other market channels.

Snails can also be exported to foreign countries, and it is a very profitable venture; just that there must be a link between the importer and the exporter. They can be exported live or processed by removing the shell and frozen before exportation. Snail meat is a delicacy and it attracts good price especially in African restaurants in the United States of America and some European countries.

In addition to the pieces of information given in this manual, seek more information to improve yourself. Do this by attending seminars or workshops on snail

breeding, buy books that extensively treat the topic, ask questions, go on visits to
individual or institutional snail farms, browse the internet so as to familiarize yourself with new technologies and put the knowledge to work. I wish you a successful venture.

For further enquires;
E-mail: aquatonkonsults@yahoo.com

ABOUT THE AUTHOR

Prince Anthony Adefarakan as he is popularly called is the M.D/CEO of Aquaton Konsults, Nigeria, West Africa. He is an experienced Snail Farming Consultant with vast wealth of knowledge in matters relating to snails production. He has practically carried out artificial snail breeding, snail rearing facilities' construction, snail feeding, and snail disease management among other snail production techniques.

He was a lecturer at Federal College of Education (Technical), Asaba where he had the opportunity to impact the Agriculture students of the institution with relevant knowledge capable of making them self-reliant upon graduation.

He currently lives in Canada with his family.

For successful snails production at all levels, this step by step handbook is a must read.

www.ingramcontent.com/pod-product-compliance
Lightning Source LLC
Chambersburg PA
CBHW071918070526
44583CB00016B/2047